# SMOOTHIES
## BEST-EVER COOL DRINK RECIPES

# SMOOTHIES
# BEST-EVER COOL DRINK RECIPES

bay books

## SODAS, CRUSHES & PUNCHES

# MELON FREEZIE

INGREDIENTS

500 g (17¹/₂ oz) rockmelon
500 g (17¹/₂ oz) honeydew melon
1 cup ice (12 ice cubes)
2 cups (500 ml/17 fl oz) orange juice

1   Remove the rind and seeds from the melons. Cut the flesh into pieces and mix in a blender for 1 minute, or until smooth.

2   Add the ice and orange juice and blend for a further 30 seconds. Transfer to a large shallow plastic dish and freeze for 3 hours.

3   Return the mixture to the blender and blend quickly until smooth. Serve immediately with straws and long spoons.

INGREDIENTS

1 lemon
1 lime
2$^1$/$_2$ tablespoons lemon juice
$^2$/$_3$ cup (170 ml/5$^3$/$_4$ fl oz) lime juice cordial
2$^1$/$_2$ cups (625 ml/21 fl oz) soda water, chilled

**1** Using a sharp knife, remove the peel and white pith from the lemon and lime. On a chopping board, cut between the membranes to release the segments. Place a lemon and lime segment in each hole of an ice cube tray and cover with water. Freeze for 2–3 hours or overnight until firm.

**2** Combine the lemon juice, lime juice cordial and soda water.

**3** Pour into long, chilled glasses with the ice cubes.

# CARROT COCKTAIL

10–12 carrots, quartered lengthways
$1/2$ cup (125 ml/4 fl oz) pineapple juice
$1/2$ cup (125 ml/4 fl oz) orange juice
1–2 teaspoons honey, to taste
8 ice cubes

**1** Using the plunger, push the carrot pieces through a juicer.

**2** Combine the carrot juice with the remaining ingredients in a jug and serve.

## INGREDIENTS

1 (2.4 kg/5$\frac{1}{2}$ lb) pineapple, peeled and cored
1 cup (250 ml/8 fl oz) ginger ale
4 scoops mandarin sorbet

1   Roughly chop the pineapple flesh then push through a juicer.

2   Combine the pineapple juice and the ginger ale in a large jug. Chill.

3   Pour the juice into chilled glasses and top with scoops of sorbet.

# GINGER LEMON AND MINT SOOTHER

2 cm (15 g/$^1/_2$ oz) piece fresh ginger, finely sliced
$^1/_2$ cup (125 ml/4 fl oz) lemon juice
2$^1/_2$ tablespoons honey
1 tablespoon fresh mint leaves

1  Place the ginger, lemon juice, honey and mint into a heatproof jug and cover with 3 cups (750 ml/25 fl oz) boiling water. Leave to infuse for 2–3 hours, or until cold.

2  When the mixture is cold, strain into another jug and chill in the refrigerator.

3  Serve in tall, chilled glasses over ice.

INGREDIENTS

4 passionfruit
100 g (3¹/₂ oz) passionfruit yoghurt
2 cups (500 ml/17 fl oz) milk
1 tablespoon caster sugar
2 scoops vanilla ice cream

**1** Scoop out the pulp from the passionfruit and push through a sieve to remove the seeds. Place into the blender with the yoghurt, milk, sugar and ice cream and blend until smooth.

**2** Pour into tall glasses and serve with an extra scoop of ice cream, if desired.

# PASSIONFRUIT AND VANILLA ICE CREAM WHIP

# CRANBERRY AND VANILLA ICE CREAM SPIDER

2 cups (500 ml/17 fl oz) cranberry juice

2 cups (500 ml/17 fl oz) soda water

4 scoops vanilla ice cream

3/4 cup (185 ml/6 1/4 fl oz) cream

1 tablespoon caster sugar

20 g (3/4 oz) flaked almonds, toasted

1 Combine the juice and soda water in a jug. Add a scoop of ice cream to each tall glass. Pour the juice and soda over the ice cream.

2 Whip the cream and sugar until soft peaks form. Spoon over the juice and soda and top with a sprinkle of almonds

INGREDIENTS

500 g ($^1/_2$ lb) rockmelon, peeled and seeded
2 tablespoons honey
1$^1/_2$ cups (375 ml) milk
5 scoops vanilla ice cream
ground nutmeg, to garnish

1   Cut the rockmelon into 2 cm (1 inch) pieces and place in a blender. Mix for 30 seconds, or until smooth.

2   Add the honey, milk and ice cream and blend for a further 10–20 seconds, or until well combined and smooth.

3   Serve sprinkled with nutmeg.

# WATERMELON SMOOTHIE

600 g (21 oz) watermelon, skinned and seeded
1 cup (250 ml/4 fl oz) milk
$1/2$ cup (125 g/$4^1/_2$ oz) yoghurt
1 tablespoon caster sugar
2 scoops vanilla ice cream

1   Blend the watermelon, milk, yoghurt and caster sugar in a blender until smooth.

2   Add the ice cream and blend for a further few seconds, or until the mixture is frothy.
Serve immediately.

INGREDIENTS

2 eggs, separated
1/4 cup (60 ml/2 fl oz) milk
1/4 cup (60 g/2 fl oz) caster sugar
1/3 cup (80 ml/2³/4 fl oz) cream
1³/4 cups (440 ml/15 fl oz) peach nectar
2 tablespoons orange juice
ground nutmeg, to garnish

1 Beat the egg yolks, milk and half the sugar in a bowl and place over a pan of simmering water—do not allow the base of the bowl to touch the water. Cook, stirring, for 8 minutes, or until the custard thickens. Remove from the heat and cover the surface with plastic wrap. Cool.

2 Beat the egg whites until frothy. Add the remaining sugar, to taste, then beat until stiff peaks form. In a separate bowl, whip the cream until soft peaks form.

3 Gently fold the egg whites and cream into the cooled custard. Stir in the nectar and juice. Cover and chill for 2 hours.

4 Beat the mixture lightly, pour into glasses and sprinkle with nutmeg.

INGREDIENTS

350 g (12 oz) rockmelon
2 peaches, peeled and sliced
150 g (5 oz) strawberries, roughly chopped
4 mint leaves
$1/2$ cup (125 ml/4 fl oz) buttermilk
$1/2$ cup (125 ml/4 fl oz) orange juice
1–2 tablespoons honey

1   Remove the rind and seeds from the melon and cut the flesh into pieces.

2   Place the rockmelon, peaches, strawberries and mint leaves in a blender and blend until smooth.

3   Add the buttermilk, orange juice and 1 tablespoon of the honey and blend to combine. Taste for sweetness and add more honey if needed.

INGREDIENTS

$1/2$ cup (125 g/4 fl oz) passionfruit pulp
$3/4$ cup (185 ml/$6^{1}/4$ fl oz) lime juice cordial
3 cups (750 ml/25 fl oz) ginger ale
crushed ice

1   Combine the pulp, cordial and ginger ale in a jug. Mix well.

2   Pour into glasses filled with crushed ice. Serve immediately.

# PEACHY KEEN

3/4 cup (185 g/6 1/4 fl oz) low-fat peach and mango yoghurt
3/4 cup (185 ml/6 1/4 fl oz) apricot nectar, chilled
1/2 cup (60 g/2 oz) fresh or frozen raspberries
1 1/2 cups (300 g/10 1/2 oz) diced fresh peaches
8 large ice cubes
fresh peach wedges, to serve

1    Place the yoghurt, nectar, fruit and ice in a blender and blend until smooth.

2    Serve with the peach wedges.

## INGREDIENTS

1³/₄ cups (440 ml/15 fl oz) coffee-flavoured soy milk, chilled
2 bananas, sliced
8 large ice cubes
1 teaspoon drinking chocolate
¹/₄ teaspoon ground cinnamon

1   Place the soy milk and sliced bananas in a blender and process until smooth.

2   With the blender running, add the ice cubes one at a time until well incorporated and the desired consistency is reached.

3   Pour into tall chilled glasses and sprinkle generously with the drinking chocolate and ground cinnamon.

# BLACKCURRANT CRUSH

3 cups (750 ml/25 fl oz) apple and blackcurrant juice
2 cups (500 ml/17 fl oz) soda water
1 tablespoon caster sugar
150 g (5 oz) blueberries
ice cubes, to serve

1   Place the apple and blackcurrant juice, soda water, sugar and blueberries into a blender and blend until smooth.

2   Serve in chilled glasses over ice.

INGREDIENTS

75 g (2$^1$/$_2$ oz) dried apricots
$^1$/$_2$ cup (125 g/4$^1$/$_2$ oz) apricot yoghurt
$^2$/$_3$ cup (170 ml/5$^3$/$_4$ fl oz) light coconut milk
1$^1$/$_4$ cups (315 ml/10$^1$/$_2$ fl oz) milk
1 tablespoon honey
1 scoop vanilla ice cream
flaked coconut, toasted, to garnish

1   Cover the apricots with boiling water and soak for 15 minutes. Drain and roughly chop.
    Place the apricots, yoghurt, coconut milk, milk, honey and ice cream in a blender and
    blend until smooth.

2   Pour into tall, chilled glasses and sprinkle with the flaked coconut.

## INGREDIENTS

2 (800 g/1³/₄ lb) fresh mangoes, peeled and seeded
¹/₂ cup (125 ml/4 fl oz) milk
1 cup (250 ml/8 fl oz) buttermilk
1 tablespoon caster sugar
2 scoops mango gelati or sorbet
50 g (1³/₄ oz) blueberries

1   Place the mango, milk, buttermilk, sugar and gelati in a blender and blend until smooth.

2   Pour into chilled glasses and serve garnished with the blueberries.

1 cup (250 g/9 oz) low-fat plain yoghurt
$1/2$ cup (125 ml/4 fl oz) skim milk
$1/2$ cup (50 g/$1^3/_4$ oz) fresh dates, pitted and chopped
2 bananas, sliced
8 ice cubes

1   Place the yoghurt, milk, dates, banana and ice cubes in a blender. Blend until the mixture
    is smooth and the ice cubes have been well incorporated.

2   Serve in chilled glasses.

BANANA DATE SMOOTHIE

## BITTER LEMON CORDIAL

Place 2 cups (500 ml/16 fl oz) lemon juice and 1 cup (250 g/9 oz) caster sugar in a pan. Stir over medium heat until the sugar has dissolved. Increase the heat and simmer rapidly, without stirring, for 6 minutes, or until the liquid reaches 85°C (185°F). Stir through $1/2$ teaspoon bitters. Pour into a new bottle and lay on its side to sterilise the lid. Refrigerate. Makes 2 cups (500 ml/16 fl oz).

## APPLE & BLACKBERRY CORDIAL

Place 2 cups (500 ml/16 fl oz) fresh apple juice, 300 g (10$1/2$ oz) frozen blackberries and 1 cup (250 g/9 oz) caster sugar in a pan. Stir over medium heat until the sugar has dissolved. Increase the heat and simmer rapidly, without stirring, for 12 minutes, or until the liquid reaches 85°C (185°F). Strain out the seeds. Pour into a new bottle and lay on its side to sterilise the lid. Refrigerate. Makes 3 cups (750 ml/25 fl oz).

Place 1 cup (250 g/9 oz) passionfruit pulp, 1 cup (250 ml/8 fl oz) water, $3/4$ cup (185 g/$6^1/_2$ oz) caster sugar and $1/4$ teaspoon coconut essence in a pan. Stir over medium heat until the sugar has dissolved. Simmer rapidly, without stirring, for 6 minutes, or until the liquid reaches 85°C (185°F). Pour into a new bottle and lay on its side to sterilise the lid. Refrigerate. Makes $1^3/_4$ cups (440 ml/15 fl oz).

Place 300 g ($10^1/_2$ oz) fresh or frozen raspberries, $3/4$ cup (185 ml/$6^1/_4$ fl oz) water and $3/4$ cup (185 g/$6^1/_2$ oz) caster sugar in a pan. Stir over medium heat until the sugar has dissolved. Increase the heat and simmer rapidly, without stirring, for 6 minutes, or until the liquid reaches 85°C (185°F). Strain and discard the seeds, then stir through 100 g ($3^1/_2$ oz) fresh or frozen raspberries. Pour into a new bottle and lay on its side to sterilise the lid. Refrigerate. Makes $1^1/_2$ cups (375 ml).

45

INGREDIENTS

3 cardamom pods
1 cup (250 ml/4 fl oz) fresh orange juice
3 strips orange rind
2 tablespoons caster sugar

1    Place the cardamom pods on a chopping board and press with the side of a large knife
     to crack them open. Place the cardamom, orange juice, rind, sugar and 2 cups (500 ml/
     16 fl oz) water in a pan and stir over medium heat for 10 minutes, or until the sugar has
     dissolved. Bring to the boil then remove from the heat.

2    Leave to infuse for 2–3 hours, or until cold. Chill in the refrigerator. Strain and serve
     over ice.

## INGREDIENTS

3 cups (750 ml/25 fl oz) tomato juice
1 tablespoon Worcestershire sauce
2 tablespoons lemon juice
$1/4$ teaspoon ground nutmeg
few drops Tabasco sauce
1 cup ice (12 ice cubes)
2 lemon slices, halved

**1** Place the tomato juice, Worcestershire sauce, lemon juice, nutmeg and Tabasco sauce in a large jug and stir until combined.

**2** Place the ice cubes in a blender and blend for 30 seconds, or until the ice is crushed down to $1/2$ cup.

**3** Pour the tomato juice mixture into serving glasses and add the crushed ice and lemon slices. Season with salt and pepper before serving.

# RUBY GRAPEFRUIT AND LEMON SORBET FIZZ

2 cups (500 ml/16 fl oz) ruby grapefruit juice
1 cup (250 ml/8 fl oz) soda water
1 tablespoon caster sugar
4 scoops lemon sorbet

1   Combine the juice, soda water and sugar in a jug. Refrigerate.

2   Pour into chilled glasses and top with a scoop of lemon sorbet.

INGREDIENTS

1 cup (200 g/7 oz) low-fat blueberry fromage fraîs
3/4 cup (185 ml/6 1/4 oz) low-fat milk
1 tablespoon maple syrup
1/2 teaspoon ground cinnamon
300 g (10 1/2 oz) frozen blueberries

**1** Combine the fromage fraîs, milk, maple syrup, cinnamon and 250 g (9 oz) blueberries in a blender until smooth.

**2** Pour into chilled glasses and top with the remaining blueberries.

# APPLE AND CINNAMON HERBAL TEA

## INGREDIENTS

4 (600 g/21 oz) golden delicious apples, roughly chopped
1 cinnamon stick
3–4 tablespoons soft brown sugar
ice cubes, to serve

1 Place the apple, cinnamon stick, brown sugar and 1 litre (4 cups) water in a pan. Bring to the boil, then reduce the heat and simmer for 10–15 minutes, or until the flavours have infused and the apples have softened.

2 Remove from the heat, cool slightly, then chill in the refrigerator until cold.

3 When cold, strain and serve over lots of ice.

INGREDIENTS

1 mango, cut into slices
2 cups (500 ml/16 fl oz) mandarin juice
$1/2$ cup (125 ml/4 fl oz) lime juice cordial
$1^1/_2$ cups (375 ml/12 fl oz) soda water
2 tablespoons caster sugar
ice cubes, to serve

1 Freeze the mango for about 1 hour, or until semi-frozen.

2 Combine the juice, cordial, soda water and sugar in a jug.

3 Place the mango slices and some ice cubes into each glass, then pour in the juice mix.

1 cup (250 g/9 oz) low-fat strawberry yoghurt
$^1/_2$ cup (125 ml/4 fl oz) cranberry juice, chilled
250 g (9 oz) strawberries, hulled and quartered
125 g (4$^1/_2$ oz) frozen raspberries

1    Combine the yoghurt and cranberry juice in a blender. Add the strawberries and 80 g
     (3 oz) of the raspberries. Blend until smooth.

2    Pour into chilled glasses and top with the remaining frozen raspberries. Serve with a spoon
     as it is quite thick.

INGREDIENTS

1 cup (250 g/8 fl oz) low-fat vanilla yoghurt
$^1/_2$ cup (125 ml/4 fl oz) buttermilk
1$^1/_4$ cups (315 ml/10$^1/_2$ fl oz) milk
1 cup (150 g/5$^1/_2$ oz) prunes, pitted and diced
$^1/_2$ cup (200 g/7 oz) diced fresh plums
8 large ice cubes

1   Place the yoghurt, buttermilk, milk, prunes, plums and ice cubes in a blender.
    Blend until the mixture is smooth and the ice cubes have been well incorporated.

2   Serve immediately.

INGREDIENTS

3 cups (750 ml/25 fl oz) soy milk, chilled
125 g (4¹/₂ oz) soft silken tofu
4 very ripe bananas, sliced
1 tablespoon honey
1 tablespoon vanilla essence
1 tablespoon carob powder (see note)

1   Combine the soy milk and tofu in a blender. Add the banana, honey, vanilla
    essence and carob powder. Blend until smooth.

2   Serve in tall chilled glasses with a long spoon.

NOTE   Carob powder is available from health food stores.

## INGREDIENTS

1 small orange
$1/2$–1 tablespoon Darjeeling tea leaves
1 cup (250 ml/8 fl oz) ginger beer
8 thin slices glacé ginger
2 tablespoons sugar
4–6 ice cubes
mint leaves, to garnish

1  Remove the peel from the orange using a vegetable peeler, avoiding the white pith, and cut into long thin strips. Place half the peel and the tea leaves in a bowl and pour in 2 cups (500 ml/16 fl oz) boiling water. Cover and leave to steep for 5 minutes, then strain through a fine strainer.

2  Pour into a jug, add the ginger beer and chill for 6 hours, or preferably overnight.

3  One hour before serving, add the ginger, sugar and remaining orange peel. Stir well.

4  Pour into tall glasses, add 2–3 ice cubes per glass and garnish with mint leaves.

ORANGE AND GINGER TEA COOLER

## INGREDIENTS

1/2 cup (110 g/4 oz) pearl barley
3 lemons
1/2 cup (125 g/41/2 oz) caster sugar
crushed ice, to serve
lemon slices, to garnish

1   Wash the barley well and place in a medium pan. Using a sharp vegetable peeler, remove the peel from the lemons, avoiding the bitter white pith. Squeeze out the juice and set aside. Add the peel and 1.75 litres (60 oz) cold water to the barley and bring to the boil. Simmer briskly for 30 minutes. Add the sugar and mix well to dissolve. Allow to cool.

2   Strain the liquid into a jug and add the lemon juice. Serve over crushed ice and garnish with lemon slices.

INGREDIENTS

400 g (14 oz) fresh mango pulp
$1/2$ cup (125 ml/4 fl oz) fresh lime juice
$1/2$ cup (125 ml/4 fl oz) coconut milk
2 teaspoons honey
3 teaspoons finely chopped fresh mint
200 g (7 oz) ice cubes

1   Place the mango pulp, lime juice, coconut milk, honey, mint and ice in a blender
    and blend until smooth.

2   Chill well and serve.

# FRUIT SPRITZER

2 cups (500 ml/16 fl oz) apricot nectar, chilled
2 cups (500 ml/16 fl oz) soda water, chilled
1 cup (250 ml/8 fl oz) apple juice, chilled
1 cup (250 ml/8 fl oz) orange juice, chilled
8 ice cubes

1 Place the apricot nectar, soda water, apple juice, orange juice and ice cubes in a large jug and stir until combined.

2 Pour into glasses and serve.

INGREDIENTS

1¹/₂ cups (375 ml/12 fl oz) very strong (double strength) fresh coffee
2 tablespoons honey
1¹/₂ cups (375 ml/12 fl oz) milk
caster sugar, to taste

**1** Pour the hot coffee into a heatproof jug and add the honey. Stir until the honey has totally dissolved, then chill in the refrigerator.

**2** Add the milk and taste for sweetness. Add a little caster sugar if necessary. Pour about ¹/₂ cup (125 ml/4¹/₄ fl oz) of the mixture into eight holes of an ice cube tray and freeze. Meanwhile, chill the remaining mixture in the refrigerator.

**3** When ready to serve, place four coffee ice cubes in each glass, then pour in the iced coffee.

# HOMEMADE LEMONADE

2$^3$/$_4$ cups (685 ml/1$^1$/$_2$ pt) lemon juice
1$^1$/$_4$ cups (310 g/11 oz) sugar
ice cubes, to serve
mint leaves, to garnish

**1** Combine the lemon juice and sugar in a large bowl, stirring until the sugar has dissolved. Pour into a large jug.

**2** Add 1.25 litres (2$^1$/$_2$ pt) water to the jug, stirring well to combine. Chill.

**3** To serve, pour over ice cubes and garnish with mint leaves.

INGREDIENTS

3 passionfruit, halved
1 large banana, chopped
1 cup (250 ml/8 fl oz) skim milk
1/4 cup (60 g/2 oz) low-fat plain yoghurt

1   Scoop out the passionfruit pulp and place in a blender. Add the banana, milk and yoghurt and blend, turning quickly on and off (or use the pulse button), until smooth and the seeds are finely chopped. (Add more milk if it is too thick.) Don't blend for too long or it will become very bubbly and increase in volume.

# SMOOTHBERRY

150 g (5$^1$/$_2$ oz) strawberries, hulled
60 g (2 oz) raspberries
200 g (7 oz) boysenberries
1 cup (250 ml/8 fl oz) milk
3 scoops vanilla ice cream

**1** Place the strawberries, raspberries, boysenberries, milk and ice cream in a blender and blend until smooth. Chill.

**2** Pour into glasses and serve.

NOTE If boysenberries are unavailable, any other berry can be used.

2 tablespoons rich chocolate topping
1¹/₂ cups (375 ml/12 fl oz) icy-cold milk
1 scoop vanilla ice cream
whipped cream, to serve
drinking chocolate, to serve

**1** Pour the chocolate topping into a glass and swirl it around the sides. Fill with the cold milk and add the ice cream.

**2** Serve with a big swirl of whipped cream and dust with drinking chocolate.

**ICED CHOCOLATE**

## PASSIONFRUIT AND MINT

Halve 8 passionfruit and divide the seeds and pulp among the ice cube holes. Place a mint leaf on top of each and fill with water. Freeze.
Delicious in pineapple juice.

## APPLE AND KIWI

Peel and cut 4 kiwi fruit each into eight wedges. Place 1 tablespoon apple juice into each ice cube hole and 2 wedges of kiwi fruit. Freeze.
Try this with ginger beer.

## STRAWBERRY

Halve 16 strawberries and place 2 halves into each ice cube hole. Top with 1 tablespoon water. Freeze.
Great in punches and cocktails.

## PINEAPPLE AND PEAR

Divide 1 cup (250 ml) pineapple juice among ice cube holes. Chop 1 unpeeled pear into pieces and place evenly into each hole. Freeze.
Serve with apricot nectar.

## LEMON, LIME AND BITTERS

Combine $1/2$ cup (125 ml/4 fl oz) lemon juice and $1/2$ cup (125 ml/4 fl oz) lime juice and divide among the ice cube holes. Add 4 drops of bitters to each hole and submerge a lime zest. Freeze. Serve in soda water.

## ORANGE AND MANGO

Pour 1 tablespoon freshly squeezed orange juice into each ice cube hole, then divide pieces from 1 mango among the tray, making sure each piece is submerged. Freeze.
Delicious in apple juice or soda water.

## GINGER ALE AND CUCUMBER

Divide 1 cup (250 ml/8 fl oz) ginger ale evenly among ice cube holes. Cut 36 thin slices from a Lebanese cucumber. Place 2 slices of cucumber in each hole. Freeze.
Gives a new twist to apple juice.

## BERRY AND MINT

Purée 150 g (5 oz) blueberries and 150 g (5 oz) raspberries until smooth, then sieve. Divide among ice cube holes. Top each hole with a mint leaf. Freeze.
Great in apple juice and soda water.

INGREDIENTS

**3 lemon grass stalks**
**2 slices lemon**
**3 teaspoons honey, or to taste**
**lemon slices, extra, to serve**

1      Prepare the lemon grass by removing the first two tough outer layers. For maximum flavour, only use the bottom one-third of the stalk (the white part). Slice thinly into rings. (You could use the remaining stalks as a garnish, if you like.)

2      Place the lemon grass in a jug and cover with 2$\frac{1}{2}$ cups (625 ml/21 fl oz) boiling water. Add the lemon slices and cover. Allow to infuse and cool. When cooled to room temperature, strain. Add the honey, to taste. Place the tea in the refrigerator to chill.

3      To serve, pour the tea into two glasses with extra slices of lemon. Add ice, if desired.

300 g fresh or frozen raspberries, thawed
1<sup>1</sup>/<sub>4</sub> cups (310 g/11 oz) sugar
2 cups (500 ml/16 fl oz) lemon juice
ice cubes, to serve
mint leaves, to garnish

**1** Combine the raspberries and sugar in a blender and blend until smooth.

**2** Place a strong sieve over a large bowl and push the mixture through to remove the seeds. Discard the seeds.

**3** Add the lemon juice and mix well. Pour into a large jug and stir in 1.5 litres (50 fl oz) water, then refrigerate until cold.

**4** To serve, pour over ice cubes and garnish with mint leaves.

# RASPBERRY LEMONADE

# RASPBERRY AND APPLE JUICE

6 Granny Smith apples, quartered
150 g (5 oz) fresh raspberries
ice cubes, to serve
mint sprigs, to garnish

**1** Using the plunger, push the apple pieces and raspberries through a juicer and into a jug. Chill.

**2** Stir well before serving. Add ice and garnish with mint sprigs.

## INGREDIENTS

1 cup (250 ml/8 fl oz) apple juice
100 g (3¹/₂ oz) papaya, peeled, seeded, chopped
200 g (7 oz) watermelon, seeded, chopped
100 g (3¹/₂ oz) ice cubes

 Blend the apple juice, papaya, watermelon and ice cubes in a blender until smooth. Chill well.

 Pour into glasses and serve.

**HAWAIIAN CRUSH**

# ICED LEMON AND PEPPERMINT TEA

2 peppermint tea bags
6 strips lemon rind (2 x 5 cm/1x 2 inches)
1 tablespoon sugar (or to taste)
ice cubes, to serve
mint leaves, to garnish

1   Place the tea bags and lemon rind strips in a large bowl. Cover with 3$\frac{1}{3}$ cups (830 ml/
    28 oz) boiling water and leave to infuse for 5 minutes.

2   Squeeze out the tea bags and discard. Stir in the sugar to taste.

3   Pour into a jug and chill. Serve in chilled glasses with ice cubes and mint leaves.

INGREDIENTS

**8 oranges**
**150 g (5 oz) baby fennel**

1    Peel and quarter the oranges, and remove any seeds. Trim the fennel and cut in half.

2    Using a juicer, push the fennel through first to release the flavours, then juice the orange. Chill well.

3    Mix together well before serving.

NOTE    When in season, the flavour will be stronger in larger, more developed fennel.

## INGREDIENTS

1 large apple, cored
6 carrots, tops removed
4 celery sticks, including leaves
6 iceberg lettuce leaves
20 English spinach leaves

1   Cut the apple, carrots and celery sticks to fit the juicer.

2   Using the plunger, push all the ingredients through the juicer and into a large jug.

3   Pour into glasses and serve with ice, if desired.

## INGREDIENTS

1 green apple, cored
$1/2$ medium honeydew melon, peeled, seeds removed
2 oranges, peeled
ice cubes, to serve

1   Cut the apple, melon and oranges into pieces to fit the juicer.

2   Using the plunger, push all the ingredients through the juicer and into a jug.

3   Pour into glasses and serve with ice.

# CELERY, TOMATO AND PARSLEY JUICE

## INGREDIENTS

1 cup (15 g/$^1/_2$ oz) fresh parsley
6 vine-ripened tomatoes, quartered
4 celery sticks, trimmed

**1** Using a juicer, push through the parsley leaves to infuse the flavour. Then juice the tomatoes and celery. Chill well.

**2** Before serving, mix together well and garnish with a stick of celery as a swizzle stick.

NOTE For extra spice, add a few drops of Tabasco and freshly ground black pepper.

INGREDIENTS

2 cups (500 ml/16 fl oz) fresh pineapple juice
1 cup (250 ml/8 fl oz) coconut milk
mint leaves, to garnish
pineapple leaves, to garnish

1   Combine the pineapple juice with the coconut milk in a large jug and mix well. Pour $\frac{1}{2}$ cup (125 ml/4 fl oz) of the mixture into 8 holes of an ice cube tray and freeze. Chill the remaining mixture in the refrigerator.

2   When the the ice cubes have frozen, pour the chilled juice mixture into 2 glasses, add the frozen cubes and garnish with mint and pineapple leaves.

# PAPAYA AND ORANGE SMOOTHIE

1 medium (650 g/23 oz) papaya
1 medium orange
6–8 ice cubes
200 g (7 oz) plain yoghurt
1–2 tablespoons caster sugar
ground nutmeg, to garnish

1   Peel the papaya and remove the seeds. Cut the flesh into cubes. Peel the orange and roughly chop the flesh.

2   Place the papaya, orange and ice in a blender and blend until smooth. Blend in the yoghurt, and add sugar, to taste.

3   Divide between two glasses, sprinkle lightly with nutmeg and serve.

NOTE   This keeps well for 6 hours in the fridge and is best in both flavour and colour when the small Fijian papaya are used. Peach or apricot flavoured yoghurt may be used for added flavour.

## INGREDIENTS

200 g (7 oz) fresh or frozen blueberries
1 cup (250 g/9 oz) plain yoghurt
1 cup (250 ml/8 fl oz) milk
1 tablespoon wheat germ
1–2 teaspoons honey, or to taste

**1** Blend together the blueberries, yoghurt, milk, wheat germ and honey until smooth.

**2** Pour into glasses and serve immediately.

NOTE Frozen blueberries are great for this recipe. No need to thaw, just throw into the blender frozen!

**BLUEBERRY STARTER**

# SPORTS SHAKE

2 cups (500 ml/16 fl oz) milk, chilled
2 tablespoons honey
2 eggs
$1/2$ teaspoon vanilla essence
1 tablespoon wheat germ
1 medium banana, sliced

1   Blend the milk, honey, eggs, vanilla, wheat germ and banana until smooth.

2   Chill well and serve.

INGREDIENTS

10-12 medium carrots
1 medium beetroot
2 medium green apples
2 English spinach leaves
2 celery sticks

**1** Cut the carrots to fit the juicer.

**2** Scrub the beetroot to ensure all the dirt is removed. Cut the beetroot and apples to fit the juicer.

**3** Using the plunger, push all the ingredients through the juicer and into a large jug.

**4** Serve chilled or over ice.

# WATERMELON BREAKFAST JUICE

4 cups (720 g/25 oz) chopped watermelon, seeded
2 tablespoons lime juice
1–2 cm (¹/₂ –1 inch) fresh ginger, grated, to taste
2 tablespoons chopped fresh mint

**1** Blend the watermelon, lime juice, ginger and mint in a blender using the pulse button (or by quickly turning the blender on and off a number of times). Be careful not to overblend or the mixture will go frothy.

**2** Divide between two glasses.

INGREDIENTS

**4 peppermint tea bags**
**$1/3$ cup (115 ml/4 fl oz) honey**
**2 cups (500 ml/16 fl oz) grapefruit juice**
**1 cup (250 ml/8 fl oz) orange juice**
**mint sprigs, to garnish**

1     Place the tea bags in a large heatproof jug and pour in 3 cups (750 ml/25 fl oz) boiling water. Allow to steep for 3 minutes, then remove and discard the bags. Stir in the honey and allow to cool.

2     Add the grapefruit and orange juice. Cover and chill in the refrigerator. Serve in glasses, garnished with fresh mint.

# SPRING CLEAN YOUR BODY

2 large cucumbers
6 medium (600 g/21 oz) carrots
1 large green apple
2 celery sticks, including leaves
1 large beetroot

**1** Remove the skin from the cucumbers. Cut the cucumbers, carrots, apple and celery into pieces to fit the juicer.

**2** Scrub the beetroot with a firm brush to remove any dirt and cut to fit the juicer.

**3** Using the plunger, push the fruit and vegetables through the juicer into a large jug.

**4** Serve chilled or with ice.

2 cups (500 ml/16 fl oz) chocolate-flavoured soy milk, chilled
125 g (4$^1$/$_2$ oz) soft silken tofu
$^1$/$_4$ cup (60 g/2 oz) smooth peanut butter
2 bananas, sliced
2 tablespoons chocolate syrup
8 large ice cubes

1    Combine the soy milk, tofu and peanut butter in a blender.

2    Add the banana, chocolate syrup and ice cubes. Blend until smooth.

**PEANUT CHOC POWER**

# DOUBLE CHOCOLATE SHAKE

Blend 1 cup (250 ml/8 fl oz) cold chocolate milk and 4 scoops chocolate ice cream in a blender until smooth.Pour into chilled glasses and decorate with grated chocolate. Makes 2 x 250 ml (8 fl oz) glasses.

# CARAMEL SHAKE

Blend 1 cup (250 ml/8 fl oz) cold milk, 2 scoops vanilla ice cream and $1/4$ cup (60 ml/2 fl oz) caramel fudge sauce in a blender until smooth. Pour into chilled glasses. Makes 2 x 250 ml (8 fl oz) glasses.

Blend 1 tablespoon strawberry flavouring, $^2/_3$ cup (170 ml/5$^3/_4$ fl oz) cold milk, $^1/_3$ cup (80 ml/ 2$^3/_4$ fl oz) cream and 2 scoops strawberry ice cream in a blender until smooth. Serve in chilled glasses.
Makes 2 x 250 ml (8 fl oz) glasses.

Blend 1 cup (250 ml/8 fl oz) cold milk, 2 tablespoons malt powder and 4 scoops vanilla ice cream in a blender until smooth. Taste, then add sugar if desired. Pour into chilled glasses and decorate with a sprinkle of drinking chocolate.
Makes 2 x 250 ml (8 fl oz) glasses.

INGREDIENTS

3 cm (1 inch) piece fresh ginger
3 ripe pears, cored, quartered, chilled
5 green apples, quartered, chilled

1   Using a juicer, juice the ginger, pear and apple together. Pour into a jug.

2   Mix together well and serve immediately.

INGREDIENTS

50 g (2 oz) fresh blueberries
100 g (3¹/₂ oz) fresh strawberries, hulled
3 cups (750 ml/25 fl oz) lemonade
2 scoops lemon sorbet

**1** Place the berries, lemonade and lemon sorbet into a blender and purée until well combined.

**2** Pour into cold glasses and serve immediately with extra berries, if desired.

# MIXED BERRY AND LEMONADE FIZZ

INGREDIENTS

**3 oranges, peeled**
**600 g (21 oz) chopped fresh pineapple**
**3¹/₂ cm (1¹/₂ inch) piece fresh ginger**

1   Cut the oranges into pieces to fit the juicer.

2   Using the plunger, push the orange pieces, pineapple and ginger through the juicer and into a jug.

3   Pour into glasses and serve with ice.

INGREDIENTS

315 ml (1¼ cups/10½ fl oz) lemon juice
1 tablespoon lemon zest
200 g (7 oz) caster sugar

1  Place the lemon juice, lemon zest and caster sugar in a small saucepan and stir over low heat for 5 minutes, or until the sugar is dissolved. Remove from the heat and leave to cool.

2  Add 500 ml (2 cups/16 fl oz) water to the juice mixture and mix together well. Pour the mixture into a shallow 30 x 20 cm (12 x 8 inch) metal container and place in the freezer until the mixture is beginning to freeze around the edges. Scrape the frozen sections back into the mixture with a fork. Repeat every 30 minutes until the mixture has even-size ice crystals. Beat the mixture with a fork just before serving. To serve, spoon the lemon granita into six chilled glasses.

INGREDIENTS

1 cup (250 g/9 oz) thick plain yoghurt
3 tablespoons honey
1 cup (250 ml/8 fl oz) milk
3 scoops vanilla ice cream

1   Blend the yoghurt and honey in a blender for 10 seconds, or until well combined. Add the milk and ice cream and blend until smooth.

2   Serve in chilled glasses.

# ORANGE ICE CREAM SODA

2 cups (500 ml/16 fl oz) freshly squeezed orange juice
1 cup (250 ml/8 fl oz) lemonade
2-4 scoops lemon sorbet

1  Combine the orange juice and lemonade in a jug. Pour into large chilled glasses, allowing enough room for the sorbet.

2  Add 1-2 scoops sorbet per glass.

INGREDIENTS

**3 oranges**
**250 g (9 oz) fresh strawberries**
**300 g (10$^1/_2$ oz) seedless grapes**
**2 peaches**

**1** Peel the oranges and cut to fit the juicer. Push through with the plunger.

**2** Wash and hull the strawberries. Push the strawberries and grapes through the juicer with the plunger.

**3** Place the peaches in a heatproof bowl and cover with boiling water. Leave for 30 seconds, then transfer to cold water. Peel away the skin. Cut the flesh from the stone and push through the juicer with the plunger.

**4** Pour into each glass and serve with long spoons.

## INGREDIENTS

**6 passionfruit, halved**
**2¹/₂ cups (625 ml/21 fl oz) lemonade**
**2-4 scoops vanilla ice cream**

1   Scoop out the passionfruit pulp into a jug—there should be about ¹/₂ cup (125 g/4¹/₂ oz). Combine the pulp with the lemonade and pour into 2 large chilled glasses—allow enough room for the ice cream.

2   Add 1–2 scoops of ice cream to each glass and serve with straws and long spoons.

INGREDIENTS

$^1/_2$ fresh pineapple, peeled and cored
1$^1/_2$ cups (375 ml/12$^1/_2$ fl oz) fresh orange juice
1 large pear, chopped
1 banana, chopped
40 g (1$^1/_2$ oz) chopped pawpaw

1   Chop the pineapple flesh into pieces and place in the blender. Add the orange juice, pear, banana and pawpaw and blend together until smooth.

2   Serve immediately.

## INGREDIENTS

150 g (5 oz) fruit (passionfruit, mango, banana, peaches, strawberries, blueberries)
1 cup (250 ml/8 fl oz) milk
2 teaspoons wheat germ
1 tablespoon honey
1/4 cup (60 g/2 oz) vanilla yoghurt
1 egg, optional
1 tablespoon malt powder

1   Blend all the ingredients in a blender for 30–60 seconds, or until well combined.

2   Pour into chilled glasses and serve immediately.

INGREDIENTS

4 Ceylon tea bags
2 tablespoons sugar
2 tablespoons lemon juice
1¹/₂ cups (375 ml/12 fl oz) dark grape juice
2 cups (500 ml/16 fl oz) orange juice
1¹/₂ cups (375 ml/12 fl oz) ginger ale
lemon slices, to serve

1 Place the tea bags in a heatproof bowl with 1 litre (34 fl oz) boiling water. Leave for 3 minutes. Remove the bags and stir in the sugar. Cool.

2 Stir in the juices. Refrigerate until cold, then add the ginger ale. Serve over ice cubes with a slice of lemon.

AMERICAN ICED TEA

## INGREDIENTS

**750 g (26¹/₂ oz) honeydew melon (about 1 whole medium fruit)**
**6 passionfruit (see note)**
**ice cubes, to serve**

1 Peel and seed the melon. Cut into pieces to fit the juicer.

2 Halve the passionfruit and scoop out the pulp.

3 Feed the melon pieces through the juicer and stir through the passionfruit pulp. Chill well.

4 Serve in a jug with lots of ice.

NOTE The amount of passionfruit pulp depends on the fruit. If the passionfruit are not juicy use one 120 g (4¹/₄ oz) can passionfruit pulp

INGREDIENTS

$^1/_3$ cup (80 ml/2$^3/_4$ fl oz) lemon juice, chilled
6 medium (1 kg/2 lb) green apples, chilled
mint leaves, to garnish

1 Pour the lemon juice into the serving jug.

2 Wash the apples and cut into smaller pieces to fit into the juicer. Using the plunger, push the apples through the juicer.

3 Add the apple juice to the lemon juice and stir well. Garnish with mint leaves and serve immediately.

NOTE This is a refreshing, slightly tart drink. If the apples and lemons are not cold, throw a handful of ice cubes into the blender and pulse.

## INGREDIENTS

1¹/₄ cups (315 ml/10¹/₂ fl oz) cold milk

¹/₂ cup (125 g/4¹/₂ oz) plain Greek-style yoghurt

2 teaspoons honey

70 g (2¹/₂ oz) chocolate honeycomb bar, roughly chopped

3 scoops vanilla ice cream

1   Blend all the ingredients in a blender until smooth.

2   Serve immediately.

## INGREDIENTS

1 cup (250 ml/8 fl oz) apple and blackcurrant juice
3/4 cup (185 ml/6 1/4 fl oz) milk
2 tablespoons plain yoghurt
3 scoops vanilla ice cream

1  Blend the juice, milk, yoghurt and ice cream in a blender until well combined and fluffy.

2  Serve immediately.

APPLE AND BLACKCURRANT SHAKE

# LAVENDER AND ROSE LEMONADE

2 lemons
15 g ($^1/_2$ oz) English lavender flowers (stripped from their stems)
$^1/_2$ cup (125 g/4$^1/_2$ oz) sugar
$^1/_2$ teaspoon rosewater

1 Using a sharp vegetable peeler, remove the peel from the lemons, avoiding the bitter white pith. Squeeze the juice and set aside. Place the lemon peel in a heatproof jug with the lavender flowers and sugar and pour in 2 cups (500 ml/16 fl oz) boiling water. Mix well.

2 Cover with plastic wrap and leave for 15 minutes. Strain, then add the lemon juice and the rosewater. Add enough cold water to make 1.5 litres. Serve well chilled. Garnish with fresh edible rose petals, if you wish.

INGREDIENTS

1¹/₂ cups (375 ml/12 fl oz) milk
³/₄ cup (185 ml/6¹/₄ fl oz) prepared custard
3 teaspoons honey
1¹/₂ teaspoons ground cinnamon
3 scoops vanilla ice cream
ground cinnamon, extra, to serve

1   Blend together the milk, custard, honey, cinnamon and ice cream until smooth and fluffy.

2   Pour into tall glasses, sprinkle with extra cinnamon and serve immediately.

CINNAMON AND CUSTARD SHAKE

INGREDIENTS

2 cups (500 ml/16 fl oz) milk
$1/4$ cup (55 g/2 oz) whole red glacé cherries
$1/4$ cup (25 g/$3/4$ oz) desiccated coconut
1 tablespoon chocolate topping
3 scoops chocolate ice cream

1     Blend together the milk, cherries, coconut, topping and ice cream until smooth and fluffy.

2     Pour into tall glasses and serve immediately.

1$^1$/$_2$ cups (375 ml/12 fl oz) cold milk
100 g (3$^1$/$_2$ oz) chocolate-covered caramel nougat bar, roughly chopped
2 teaspoons chocolate topping
4 scoops chocolate ice cream

**1** Blend the milk, chocolate bar, chocolate topping and ice cream together until smooth.

**2** Serve immediately.

NOTE There will still be some small pieces of chocolate after blending.

# CHOC CARAMEL SMOOTHIE

## PINEAPPLE & PAWPAW PUNCH

Peel a 2 kg (4¹/₂ lb) fresh pineapple and remove the centre core. Roughly chop the flesh. Juice the pineapple in a juicer and place in a blender with 600 g (221 oz) pawpaw. Blend until smooth. Add 1 cup (250 ml/8 fl oz) chilled ginger ale and pour into chilled glasses. Serve immediately. Garnish with extra slices of pineapple.
Makes 4 x 250 ml (8 fl oz) glasses

## PINEAPPLE DELIGHT

Peel a 750 g (26¹/₂ oz) fresh pineapple and remove the centre core. Cut the flesh into 2 cm (1 inch) pieces and blend in a blender for 1–2 minutes, or until as smooth as possible. Pour 2 cups (500 ml/16 fl oz) lemonade into a jug and add the pineapple purée, stirring gently to combine. Add 2 tablespoons lime juice and mix well. Pour into the serving glasses and garnish with mint leaves.
Makes 4 x 250 ml (8 fl oz) glasses

Place 1 cup (250 ml/8 fl oz) pineapple juice, 2 cups (500 ml/16 fl oz) orange juice, 2 cups (500 ml/16 fl oz) apple cider and 2 cups (500 ml/16 fl oz) ginger ale in a jug and stir. Scoop out the flesh from 2 passionfruit and stir into the juice. Garnish with 2 slices orange, halved and 2 slices lemon, halved.
Makes 6 x 250 ml (8 fl oz) glasses

**BERRY & CHERRY PUNCH**

Using a vegetable peeler, remove the skin from 1 lemon, avoiding the bitter white pith. Cut into long thin strips. Remove the stones from 375 g (13 oz) cherries and place the cherries in a jug. Add 200 g (7 oz) blackberries, 200 g (7 oz) blueberries, 125 g (4$\frac{1}{2}$ oz) strawberries, halved, 3 cups (750 ml/1$\frac{1}{2}$ pt) ginger ale, 2 cups (500 ml/16 fl oz) lemonade, 1 cup (250 ml/8 fl oz) cold black tea, the lemon rind and 10 coarsely torn mint leaves. Cover the jug and chill for at least 3 hours. Add ice cubes to serve.
Makes 10 x 250 ml (8 fl oz) glasses

INGREDIENTS

140 ml (4³/₄ fl oz) can coconut milk
1 cup (250 ml/8 fl oz) milk
¹/₄ cup (25 g/³/₄ oz) desiccated coconut
¹/₄ teaspoon vanilla essence
3 scoops vanilla ice cream
170 g (6 oz) can passionfruit pulp in syrup

1   Blend together the coconut milk, milk, coconut, vanilla, ice cream and half the passionfruit
    pulp until smooth and fluffy.

2   Stir in the remaining pulp and serve immediately.

## INGREDIENTS

1 cinnamon stick
1 tablespoon Earl Grey tea leaves
1 cup (250 ml/8 fl oz) orange juice
2 teaspoons finely grated orange rind
2 tablespoons sugar, to taste
ice cubes, to serve
1 orange, sliced into thin rounds
4 cinnamon sticks, extra, to garnish

1   Place the cinnamon stick, tea leaves, orange juice, orange rind and 3 cups (750 ml/25 fl oz) water in a medium pan.

2   Slowly bring to a simmer over gentle heat. Once simmering, stir in the sugar, to taste, and stir until dissolved. Remove from the heat and allow to cool. Once the mixture has cooled, strain the liquid into a jug and refrigerate until cold.

3   Serve in a jug with lots of ice cubes, and garnish with the orange slices and extra cinnamon stick.

# MINT JULIP

1 cup (20 g/³/₄ oz) fresh mint leaves
1 tablespoon sugar
1 tablespoon lemon juice
1 cup (250 ml/8 fl oz) pineapple juice
1 cup (250 ml/8 fl oz) ginger ale
ice cubes, to serve
mint leaves, to garnish

1  Roughly chop the mint leaves and place in a heatproof jug with the sugar. Using a wooden spoon, bruise the mint. Add the lemon juice, pineapple juice and ¹/₂ cup (125 ml/4 fl oz) boiling water. Mix well. Cover with plastic wrap and leave for 30 minutes.

2  Strain, then refrigerate until cold.

3  Just before serving, add the ginger ale and mix well. Serve in glasses over ice and garnish with mint leaves.

INGREDIENTS

4 apricots, halved and stoned
2 peaches, halved and stoned
1 cup (250 ml/8 fl oz) apricot nectar, chilled
150 g (5 oz) silken tofu

1   Place the apricots, peaches, nectar and tofu in a blender and blend until smooth.

2   Pour into glasses and serve.

APRICOT TOFU SMOOTHIE

## INGREDIENTS

4 ripe pears, peeled and cored
3 teaspoons caster sugar
2 teaspoons roughly chopped fresh mint
30 ice cubes
mint leaves, extra, to garnish

1   Chop the pear flesh into pieces. Place in a blender with the sugar and mint and blend until smooth.

2   Add the ice cubes and blend until smooth.

3   Serve immediately, garnished with the extra mint leaves.

1 cup (250 ml/8 fl oz) milk
1$1/4$ tablespoons chocolate syrup
5 scoops chocolate ice cream
35 g (1$1/4$ oz) chocolate-coated peppermint crisp bar, roughly chopped
1 tablespoon chopped fresh mint
5 scoops vanilla ice cream

**1** Blend half the milk with the chocolate syrup and chocolate ice cream. Pour into 4 glasses.

**2** Blend the peppermint crisp bar with the remaining milk, mint and vanilla ice cream. Pour over the chocolate mixture and swirl together to combine.

**3** Serve immediately with a straw.

# DECADENT SWIRLED CHOCOLATE THICKSHAKE

# COCONUT AND LIME LASSI

400 ml (13$^1$/$_2$ fl oz) coconut milk
$^3$/$_4$ cup (185 g/6$^1$/$_2$ oz) plain yoghurt
$^1$/$_4$ cup (60 ml/2 fl oz) fresh lime juice
$^1$/$_4$ cup (60 g/2 oz) caster sugar
8–10 ice cubes
lime slices, to garnish

1   Blend together the coconut milk, yoghurt, lime juice, sugar and ice cubes until the mixture is well combined and the ice cubes are well crushed.

2   Pour into tall glasses and serve immediately, garnished with slices of fresh lime.

INGREDIENTS

100 g (3$^1$/$_2$ oz) chopped fresh pineapple
$^1$/$_2$ small papaya, seeded and chopped
2 small bananas, sliced
$^1$/$_4$ cup (60 ml/2 fl oz) coconut milk
1 cup (250 ml/8 fl oz) orange juice
ice cubes, to serve

1   Cut the pineapple and papaya into smaller chunks and place in a blender. Add the banana
    and coconut milk and blend until smooth. Add the orange juice and blend until combined.

2   Pour into glasses and serve with ice.

# SUMMER STRAWBERRY SMOOTHIE

1 tablespoon strawberry flavouring
1 cup (250 ml/8 fl o z) wildberry drinking yoghurt
250 g (9 oz) strawberries, hulled
4 scoops frozen strawberry yoghurt
few drops vanilla essence
ice cubes, to serve

1   Combine the strawberry flavouring, drinking yoghurt, strawberries, frozen yoghurt and vanilla in a blender and process until smooth.

2   Pour over lots of ice to serve.

INGREDIENTS

1/2 cup (125 ml/4 fl oz) cold milk
50 g (1 3/4 oz) dark chocolate, grated
2 tablespoons chocolate syrup
2 tablespoons cream
4 scoops chocolate ice cream
2 scoops chocolate ice cream, extra
grated dark chocolate, extra, to serve

1   Blend the milk, chocolate, syrup, cream and ice cream in a blender until smooth.

2   Pour into chilled glasses. Top each glass with a scoop of ice cream and sprinkle with grated chocolate.

# WATERMELON GRANITA

**250 g (1 cup/9 oz) caster sugar**
**1.5 kg (53 oz) watermelon**

**1** Place the sugar in a saucepan with 250 ml (1 cup/8 fl oz) water and stir over low heat without boiling until the sugar has completely dissolved. Increase the heat and bring to the boil, then reduce the heat and simmer, without stirring, for 5 minutes. Pour into a large bowl to cool.

**2** Remove the rind from the watermelon and place chunks of flesh in a food processor. Process until puréed, then strain to remove the seeds and fibre. Mix the watermelon purée with the sugar syrup, and pour into a shallow metal dish. Freeze for 1 hour, or until just frozen around the edges. Scrape this back into the mixture with a fork.

**3** Repeat scraping the frozen edges every hour, at least twice more, or until the mixture has even-sized ice crystals. Serve immediately or beat well with a fork and refreeze just before serving. To serve, scrape the granita into serving dishes with a fork, or serve in scoops in a tall glass.

All our recipes are thoroughly tested in a specially developed test kitchen. Standard metric measuring cups and spoons are used in the development of our recipes. All cup and spoon measurements are level. We have used 60 g (2¼ oz/Grade 3) eggs in all recipes. Sizes of cans vary from manufacturer to manufacturer and between countries – use the can size closest to the one suggested in the recipe.

## CONVERSION GUIDE

1 cup = 250 ml (9 fl oz)

1 teaspoon = 5 ml

1 Australian tablespoon = 20 ml (4 teaspoons)

1 UK/US tablespoon = 15 ml (3 teaspoons)

| DRY MEASURES | LIQUID MEASURES | LINEAR MEASURES |
|---|---|---|
| 30 g = 1 oz | 30 ml = 1 fl oz | 6 mm = ¼ inch |
| 250 g = 9 oz | 125 ml = 4 fl oz | 1 cm = ½ inch |
| 500 g = 1 lb 2 oz | 250 ml = 9 fl oz | 2.5 cm = 1 inch |

## CUP CONVERSIONS – DRY INGREDIENTS

1 cup almonds, slivered whole = 125 g (4½ oz)

1 cup cheese, lightly packed processed cheddar = 155 g (5½ oz)

1 cup wheat flour = 125 g (4½ oz)

1 cup wholemeal flour = 140 g (5 oz)

1 cup minced (ground) meat = 250 g (9 oz)

1 cup pasta shapes = 125 g (4½ oz)

1 cup raisins = 170 g (6 oz)

1 cup rice, short grain, raw = 200 g (7 oz)

1 cup sesame seeds = 160 g (6 oz)

1 cup split peas = 250 g (9 oz)

## INTERNATIONAL GLOSSARY

| | |
|---|---|
| capsicum | sweet bell pepper |
| chick pea | garbanzo bean |
| chilli | chile, chili pepper |
| cornflour | cornstarch |
| eggplant | aubergine |
| spring onion | scallion |
| zucchini | courgette |
| plain flour | all-purpose flour |
| prawns | shrimp |
| minced meat | ground meat |

Where temperature ranges are indicated, the lower figure applies to gas ovens, the higher to electric ovens. This allows for the fact that the flame in gas ovens generates a drier heat, which effectively cooks food faster than the moister heat of an electric oven, even if the temperature setting is the same.

| | °C | °F | GAS MARK |
|---|---|---|---|
| Very slow | 120 | 250 | ½ |
| Slow | 150 | 300 | 2 |
| Mod slow | 160 | 325 | 3 |
| Moderate | 180 | 350 | 4 |
| Mod hot | 190(g)–210(e) | 375–425 | 5 |
| Hot | 200(g)–240(e) | 400–475 | 6 |
| Very hot | 230(g)–260(e) | 450–525 | 8 |

Published in 2006 by Bay Books,
an imprint of Murdoch Books Pty Limited.

ISBN 1-74045-939-3
978-1-74045-939-6

Printed by Sing Cheong Printing Company Ltd.
Printed in China.